FAMILY
FILL-IN BOOK

———●———

FAMILY
FILL-IN BOOK

—●—

Dian Dincin Buchman

SCHOLASTIC INC.

New York   Toronto   London   Auckland   Sydney

ISBN 0-590-46412-4

12 11 10 9 8 7 6 5 4 3 2 1

4 5 6 7 8/9
09

Printed in the U.S.A.

First Scholastic printing, January 1994

MY NAME:

_____

DATE THIS RECORD BEGINS:

_____

Me

About Me

I am _____ years old.

I am named after _____.

My name means _____.

Sometimes I am also called _____.

I got this nickname because _____.

I was born in _____
                             (city/town)   (state)   (country)

on _____
      (date)

at _____.
      (time)

_____ delivered me.
    (name)

_____ was at the hospital when I was born.
    (name)

My school is _____.

I am in the _____ grade.

My teacher's name is _____.

About Me

There are _____ other children in my family.

I am the _____ child.

       (first, second, etc.)

My brothers and sisters (include half or stepsiblings):

NAME   AGE

_____

_____

_____

_____

_____

_____

_____

_____

_____

_____

About Me

My favorite game is

_____.

My favorite song is

_____.

My best friend is

_____.

My favorite movie is

_____.

My favorite TV show is

_____.

My pet's name is

_____.

My favorite book is

_____.

My favorite food is

_____.

My favorite place is

_____.

My favorite school subject is

_____.

I Live With

NAME   HOW RELATED

_____

_____

_____

_____

_____

_____

_____

Sometimes
I Also Live With

NAME   HOW RELATED

_____

_____

_____

_____

_____

_____

_____

We Live

(Put a check mark next to your choices and fill in the blanks.)

IN THE COUNTRY:

____ On a farm

____ In the woods

____ On a body of water

____ In a trailer

____ In a house

____ In a cabin

____ Other (type of dwelling) _____

    The place we live in has _____ rooms.

IN THE CITY:

____ In a house

    The house has _____ floors, and _____ rooms.

____ In an apartment

    The apartment building has _____ floors.

    We live on the _____ floor.

    The apartment has _____ rooms.

IN THE SUBURBS:

____ In a house

    The house has _____ floors, and _____ rooms.

____ In an apartment

    The apartment building has _____ floors.

    We live on the _____ floor.

    The apartment has _____ rooms.

____ In a trailer   The trailer has _____ rooms.

____ On a boat   The boat sleeps _____.

My Mom
and Her Side
of the Family

———●———

(Fill out this section with your Mom.)

My Mom

My mother's name is _____.

I call my mother _____.
                               (nickname)

My mother was born in

_____
      (city/town)   (state)   (country)

on_____.
     (date)

If born outside the United States:

    Her nationality was _____.

    Her first language was _____.

    She grew up in _____.

    She came to America in _____.
                         (date)

MY MOTHER'S SCHOOLS:

Elementary _____

High school _____

College _____

How Long Have We Been Here? (Mom's Side of the Family)

How long has your side of the family been in the United States?

_____

_____

_____

Who were the first relatives to come here?

_____

_____

_____

Where did they come from?

_____

_____

_____

What language did they speak?

_____

Mom's Brothers and Sisters

NAME	AGE	CITY THEY LIVE IN
_____	_____	_____
_____	_____	_____
_____	_____	_____
_____	_____	_____
_____	_____	_____
_____	_____	_____
_____	_____	_____
_____	_____	_____

Which brother(s) or sister(s) is your mother closest to? _____
_____

Why?_____

When your mother was young, what were the things she liked to do with her sister(s) or brothers(s)? _____
_____
_____

Does she have a favorite memory she would like to share?

_____
_____
_____
_____
_____

My Mom and Her Mother

My grandmother's name is _____.

I call my grandmother _____.
                              (nickname)

My grandmother was born in

_____
     (city/town)   (state)   (country)

on _____.
        (date)

If born outside the United States:

    Her nationality was _____.

    Her first language was _____.

    She grew up in _____.

    She came to America in _____.
                                              (date)

My grandmother's sisters and brothers:

_____

_____

_____

_____

Place and date my grandmother and grandfather were married:

_____

My grandmother's parents (my great-grandparents)

Her mother's name: _____

Her father's name: _____

My Mom and Her Father

My grandfather's name is _____.

I call my grandfather _____.
                           (nickname)
My grandfather was born in

_____
     (city/town)   (state)   (country)
on_____.
        (date)

If born outside the United States:

    His nationality was _____.

    His first language was _____.

    He grew up in _____.

    He came to America in _____.
                                        (date)

My grandfather's sisters and brothers:

_____

_____

_____

_____

My grandfather's parents (my great-grandparents)

His mother's name: _____

His father's name: _____

My Family Roots
(Mom's Side of the Family)

ME   MOM

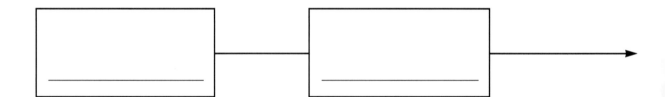

GRANDPARENTS

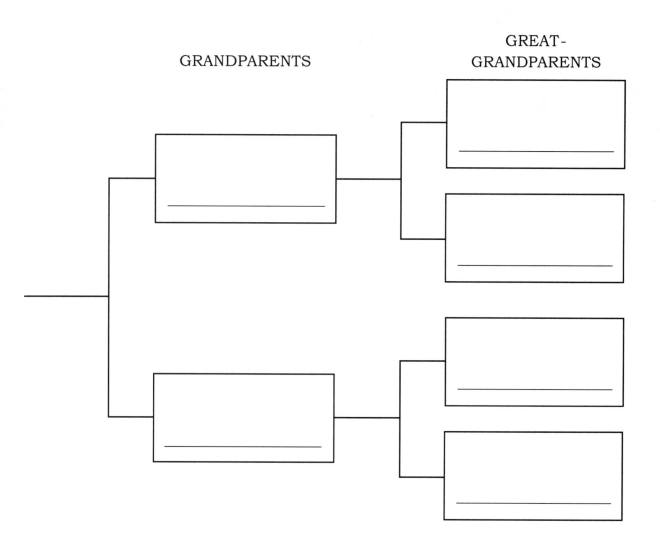

The Journey Here
(Mom's Side of the Family)

The first relatives who came here traveled by _____.

City or port of departure: _____

City or port of arrival: _____

If by ship, name: _____

Why did they come? _____
_____

Where did they stop on the way? _____
_____

How much money did they have when they arrived? _____

What did they bring with them? _____
_____

Are there any interesting stories about their arrival?

_____
_____
_____
_____
_____
_____

Did anyone meet them when they arrived? Who? _____
_____

Are there any pictures of these early relatives? _____

Does anyone have letters, pictures, trunks, or clothing that belonged to them?
_____

Where Your Family Settled (Mom's Side)

To which parts of the United States did your first relatives go? _____

_____

_____

_____

In what other parts of the United States did your relatives settle? _____

_____

_____

_____

_____

Did most of them stay in one place? _____

_____

If the family wandered around a lot, in which states, cities, and towns did they end up? _____

_____

_____

_____

_____

Why did they move? _____

_____

_____

_____

_____

The Kind of Work
You and Your Family Did
(Mom's Side)

What kind of work did your relatives do before they came to America? _____
_____

When your first relatives arrived here, what kind of work did they do? _____
_____

About how much money did they make at that time? _____
_____

What kind of work did your grandfather do? _____
_____

What kind of work did your grandmother do? _____
_____

What kind of work did your father do? _____
_____

Did he like his job? Why? _____
_____

What kind of work did your mother do? _____
_____

Did she like her job? Why? _____
_____

Did any members of your family join or organize a union? Which one?
_____

Mom as a Kid

—CHILDHOOD—

What word would you use to describe yourself as a child? _____

Describe your childhood in one sentence. _____

_____

Where did you grow up? _____

—EVERYDAY LIFE—

As a kid, did you have jobs to do around the house? Outside the house? _____

Did you get paid? About how much? _____

What was dinnertime like when you were a kid? Did you laugh or talk about the day? Did you all sit down to eat together? Were you a picky eater? _____

_____

_____

_____

_____

What things did you like to do with your mom? Your dad? _____

_____

_____

—FAVORITES—

Did you have a favorite pet? What was its name? _____

What was your favorite movie? _____

What was your favorite television show? _____

Who was your favorite musical group? _____

What did you like best about the summer? Winter? _____

_____

_____

What was your favorite food? _____

What were your favorite outdoor and indoor games? _____

_____

What was your favorite book as a child? _____

As a teenager? _____

What did you worry about when you were a kid? _____

_____

—DRESS AND HAIR—

What kind of clothes did you wear to school? Was there a dress code?

_____

How differently did you dress from girls now?

In elementary school: _____

In high school: _____

How did you wear your hair in elementary school? _____

_____

In high school? _____

_____

—SCHOOL DAYS—

ELEMENTARY SCHOOL:

What was your best time? _____

_____

What was your worst time? _____

_____

What were your best and worst subjects? _____

_____

Who were your friends? _____

_____

Are you still friendly with any of them? _____

_____

HIGH SCHOOL:

Was high school fun for you? In what way? _____

_____

Did you participate in any sports? Which ones? _____

_____

Did you belong to any clubs? Which ones? _____

_____

_____

What were the subjects you liked? Why? _____

_____

_____

COLLEGE:

What do you remember most about college? _____

_____

_____

—DREAMS—

As a child, what did you want to be when you grew up? _____

_____

What were your dreams or special goals for yourself when you were
a teenager? _____

_____

Do you remember a special time when you felt successful? _____

_____

_____

Name a teacher or a family friend who was important in your life. How was this
person important? _____

_____

What are some accomplishments you are proud of? _____

_____

Meeting Dad

How did you meet Dad? _____

_____

_____

How old were you? _____

What did you like about him? Was it love at first sight? _____

_____

_____

Tell me about your first date with Dad. _____

_____

_____

_____

Tell me about other dates you remember. _____

_____

_____

_____

Did you go dancing? _____

_____

_____

Were you working when you met Dad? _____

What kind of work did you do then? _____

_____

_____

The Wedding

Do you remember the moment you and Dad decided to get married? _____

_____

_____

Did your parents like Dad? _____

Was there a formal proposal? Describe. _____

_____

_____

Were there any special parties for you? Describe. _____

_____

_____

When and where were you married? _____

_____

What was your wedding like? Where was it held? How many people were invited?

_____

_____

What kind of wedding dress did you wear? What hat? What veil? What shoes?
Gloves? Did you carry flowers? _____

_____

_____

Who performed the ceremony? _____

Was it a formal ceremony? Did you write any of it? _____

Did anything unusual or funny happen at the wedding? _____

_____

What kind of food did you have at the wedding? _____

_____

What kind of music was played at your wedding? _____

_____

Starting Out

Did you start out with all the things you needed for your home, or did you have to work hard to get those things? _____

_____

_____

_____

Where was your first home together? Describe it. _____

_____

_____

What kind of work did you do after you were married? _____

_____

_____

—WHEN I WAS BORN—

When I was born who helped take care of me? _____

_____

What was the best thing about being a mom? _____

_____

_____

What was the most difficult thing about being a mom? _____

_____

_____

_____

My Dad
and His Side
of the Family

———●———

(Fill out this section with your Dad.)

My Dad

My father's name is _____.

I call my father _____.
              (nickname)

My father was born in

_____

        (city/town)   (state)   (country)

on _____.

      (date)

If born outside the United States:

  His nationality was _____.

  His first language was _____.

  He grew up in _____.

  He came to America in _____.

                    (date)

MY FATHER'S SCHOOLS:

Elementary _____

High school _____

College _____

How Long Have We Been Here?
(Dad's Side of the Family)

How long has your side of the family been in the United States?

_____

_____

_____

Who were the first relatives to come here?

_____

_____

_____

Where did they come from?

_____

_____

_____

What language did they speak?

_____

Dad's Brothers and Sisters

NAME   AGE   CITY THEY LIVE IN

_____

_____

_____

_____

_____

_____

_____

_____

Which brother(s) or sister(s) is your father closest to? _____

_____

Why? _____

When your father was young, what were the things he liked to do with his
sister(s) or brothers(s)? _____

_____

_____

Does he have a favorite memory he would like to share?

_____

_____

_____

_____

My Dad and His Mother

My grandmother's name is _____.

I call my grandmother _____.
                                     (nickname)

My grandmother was born in

_____
   (city/town)   (state)   (country)

on_____.
       (date)

If born outside the United States:

    Her nationality was _____.

    Her first language was _____.

    She grew up in _____.

    She came to America in _____.
                            (date)

My grandmother's sisters and brothers:

_____

_____

_____

_____

Place and date my grandmother and grandfather were married:

_____

My grandmother's parents (my great-grandparents)

Her mother's name: _____

Her father's name: _____

My Dad and His Father

My grandfather's name is _____.

I call my grandfather _____.
              (nickname)

My grandfather was born in

_____

   (city/town)   (state)   (country)

on_____.
   (date)

If born outside the United States:

   His nationality was _____.

   His first language was _____.

   He grew up in _____.

   He came to America in _____.
                  (date)

My grandfather's sisters and brothers:

_____

_____

_____

_____

My grandfather's parents (my great-grandparents)

His mother's name: _____

His father's name: _____

My Family Roots
(Dad's Side of the Family)

ME   DAD

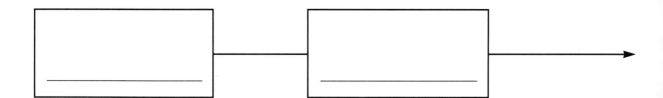

GRANDPARENTS

GREAT-
GRANDPARENTS

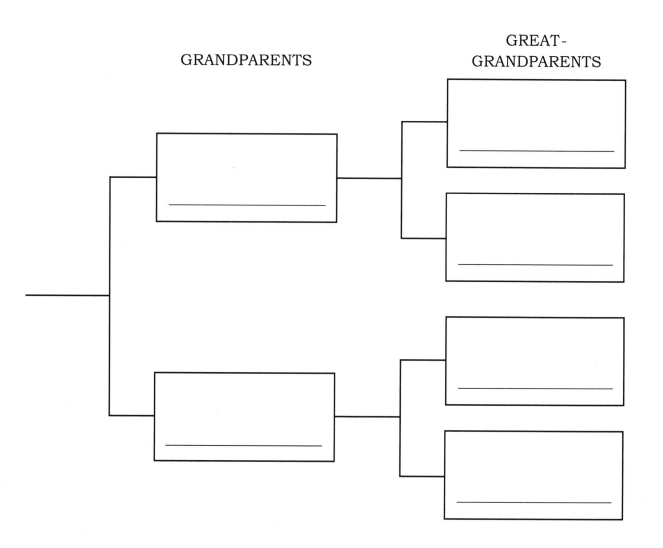

The Journey Here
(Dad's Side of the Family)

The first relatives who came here traveled by _____.

City or port of departure: _____

City or port of arrival: _____

If by ship, name: _____

Why did they come? _____
_____

Where did they stop on the way? _____
_____

How much money did they have when they arrived? _____

What did they bring with them? _____
_____

Are there any interesting stories about their arrival?
_____
_____
_____
_____
_____
_____
_____

Did anyone meet them when they arrived? Who? _____
_____

Are there any pictures of these early relatives? _____

Does anyone have letters, pictures, trunks, or clothing that belonged to them?
_____

Where Your Family Settled
(Dad's Side)

To which parts of the United States did your first relatives go? _____

_____

_____

_____

In what other parts of the United States did your relatives settle? _____

_____

_____

_____

_____

Did most of them stay in one place? _____

_____

If the family wandered around a lot, in which states, cities, and towns did they end up? _____

_____

_____

_____

Why did they move? _____

_____

_____

_____

_____

The Kind of Work
You and Your Family Did
(Dad's Side)

What kind of work did your relatives do before they came to America? _____

_____

When your first relatives arrived here, what kind of work did they do? _____

_____

About how much money did they make at that time? _____

_____

What kind of work did your grandfather do? _____

_____

What kind of work did your grandmother do? _____

_____

What kind of work did your father do? _____

_____

Did he like his job? Why? _____

_____

What kind of work did your mother do? _____

_____

Did she like her job? Why? _____

_____

Did any members of your family join or organize a union? Which one? _____

_____

Dad as a Kid

—CHILDHOOD—

What word would you use to describe yourself as a child? _____

Describe your childhood in one sentence. _____

_____

Where did you grow up? _____

—EVERYDAY LIFE—

As a kid, did you have jobs to do around the house? Outside the house? _____

Did you get paid? About how much? _____

What was dinnertime like when you were a kid? Did you laugh or talk about
the day? Did you all sit down to eat together? Were you a picky eater? _____

_____

_____

_____

_____

What things did you like to do with your mom? Your dad? _____

_____

_____

—FAVORITES—

Did you have a favorite pet? What was its name? _____

What was your favorite movie? _____

What was your favorite television show? _____

Who was your favorite musical group? _____

What did you like best about the summer? Winter? _____

_____

_____

What was your favorite food? _____

What were your favorite outdoor and indoor games? _____
_____

What was your favorite book as a child? _____

As a teenager? _____

What did you worry about when you were a kid? _____
_____

—DRESS AND HAIR—

What kind of clothes did you wear to school? Was there a dress code?
_____

How differently did you dress from boys now?

In elementary school: _____

In high school: _____

How did you wear your hair in elementary school? _____
_____

In high school? _____
_____

—SCHOOL DAYS—

ELEMENTARY SCHOOL:

What was your best time? _____
_____

What was your worst time? _____
_____

What were your best and worst subjects? _____
_____

Who were your friends? _____
_____

Are you still friendly with any of them? _____
_____

HIGH SCHOOL:

Was high school fun for you? In what way? _____

_____

Did you participate in any sports? Which ones? _____

_____

Did you belong to any clubs? Which ones? _____

_____

_____

What were the subjects you liked? Why? _____

_____

_____

COLLEGE:

What do you remember most about college? _____

_____

_____

—DREAMS—

As a child, what did you want to be when you grew up? _____

_____

What were your dreams or special goals for yourself when you were
a teenager? _____

_____

Do you remember a special time when you felt successful? _____

_____

_____

Name a teacher or a family friend who was important in your life. How was this
person important? _____

_____

What are some accomplishments you are proud of? _____

_____

Meeting Mom

How did you meet Mom? _____

_____

_____

How old were you? _____

What did you like about her? Was it love at first sight? _____

_____

_____

Tell me about your first date with Mom. _____

_____

_____

_____

Tell me about other dates you remember. _____

_____

_____

_____

Did you go dancing? _____

_____

_____

Were you working when you met Mom? _____

What kind of work did you do then? _____

_____

_____

The Wedding

Do you remember the moment you and Mom decided to get married?

_____

_____

Did your parents like Mom? _____

Was there a formal proposal? Describe. _____

_____

Were there any special parties for you? Describe. _____

_____

_____

What do you remember about the wedding? _____

_____

_____

_____

Did anything unusual or funny happen at the wedding? _____

_____

_____

_____

Starting Out

Did you start out with all the things you needed for your home, or did you have to work hard to get those things? _____

_____

_____

_____

Where was your first home together? Describe it. _____

_____

_____

_____

What kind of work did you do after you were married? _____

_____

_____

—WHEN I WAS BORN—

When I was born who helped take care of me? _____

_____

What was the best thing about being a dad? _____

_____

_____

_____

What was the most difficult thing about being a dad? _____

_____

_____

_____

My Grandparents

———●———

(Fill out this section with your grandparents. If they aren't available, ask your parents or another relative to help you.)

Grandmother
(My Mom's Mother)

Name: _____

What are your parents' names? _____

_____

What are your grandparents' names? _____

_____

Did you live near your grandparents? _____

Do you have any brothers and/or sisters? List their names. _____

_____

_____

—CHILDHOOD—

Describe your childhood in one sentence. _____

_____

What is one of your earliest memories? _____

_____

What kind of games did you play when you were a kid? _____

_____

Do you remember a joke you told as a kid? _____

_____

_____

What was your favorite song? (Ask her to sing it to you.) _____

_____

Do you have a favorite holiday? Why? _____

_____

Do you remember where you were when President John F. Kennedy was killed? Explain. _____

_____

Grandfather
(My Mom's Father)

Name: _____

What are your parents' names? _____

_____

What are your grandparents' names? _____

_____

Did you live near your grandparents? _____

Do you have any brothers and/or sisters? List their names. _____

_____

_____

—CHILDHOOD—

Describe your childhood in one sentence. _____

_____

What is one of your earliest memories? _____

_____

What kind of games did you play when you were a kid? _____

_____

Do you remember a joke you told as a kid? _____

_____

_____

What was your favorite song? (Ask him to sing it to you.) _____

_____

Do you have a favorite holiday? Why? _____

_____

Do you remember where you were when President John F. Kennedy was killed?
Explain. _____

_____

Grandmother
(My Dad's Mother)

Name: _____

What are your parents' names? _____

_____

What are your grandparents' names? _____

_____

Did you live near your grandparents? _____

Do you have any brothers and/or sisters? List their names. _____

_____

_____

—CHILDHOOD—

Describe your childhood in one sentence. _____

_____

What is one of your earliest memories? _____

_____

What kind of games did you play when you were a kid? _____

_____

Do you remember a joke you told as a kid? _____

_____

_____

What was your favorite song? (Ask her to sing it to you.) _____

_____

Do you have a favorite holiday? Why? _____

_____

Do you remember where you were when President John F. Kennedy was killed?
Explain. _____

_____

Grandfather
(My Dad's Father)

Name: _____

What are your parents' names? _____

_____

What are your grandparents' names? _____

_____

Did you live near your grandparents? _____

Do you have any brothers and/or sisters? List their names. _____

_____

_____

—CHILDHOOD—

Describe your childhood in one sentence. _____

_____

What is one of your earliest memories? _____

_____

What kind of games did you play when you were a kid? _____

_____

Do you remember a joke you told as a kid? _____

_____

_____

What was your favorite song? (Ask him to sing it to you.) _____

_____

Do you have a favorite holiday? Why? _____

_____

Do you remember where you were when President John F. Kennedy was killed?
Explain. _____

_____

My Great-Grandparents
(Mom's Side)

(MY MATERNAL GRANDMOTHER'S PARENTS)

My grandmother's parents' names: _____

My great-grandmother was born in

_____ on _____.

    (city/town)   (state)   (country)   (date)

If born outside the United States:

    Her nationality was _____.

    Her first language was _____.

    She grew up in _____.

    If she came to America, when did she arrive? _____

    Where? _____

My great-grandfather was born in

_____ on _____.

(city/town)   (state)   (country)   (date)

If born outside the United States:

    His nationality was _____.

    His first language was _____.

    He grew up in _____.

    If he came to America, when did he arrive? _____

    Where? _____

Place and date my great-grandparents were married: _____

When my grandmother was born they lived in

_____.

    (city/town)   (state)   (country)

My Great-Grandparents (Mom's Side)

(MY MATERNAL GRANDFATHER'S PARENTS)

My grandfather's parents' names: _____

My great-grandmother was born in

_____ on _____.
   (city/town)   (state)   (country)   (date)

If born outside the United States:

   Her nationality was _____.

   Her first language was _____.

   She grew up in _____.

   If she came to America, when did she arrive? _____

   Where? _____

My great-grandfather was born in

_____ on _____.
   (city/town)   (state)   (country)   (date)

If born outside the United States:

   His nationality was _____.

   His first language was _____.

   He grew up in _____.

   If he came to America, when did he arrive? _____

   Where?_____

Place and date my great-grandparents were married: _____

When my grandfather was born they lived in

_____.
   (city/town)   (state)   (country)

My Great-Grandparents (Dad's Side)

(MY PATERNAL GRANDMOTHER'S PARENTS)

My grandmother's parents' names: _____

My great-grandmother was born in

_____ on _____.
   (city/town)   (state)   (country)   (date)

If born outside the United States:

   Her nationality was _____.

   Her first language was _____.

   She grew up in _____.

   If she came to America, when did she arrive? _____

   Where? _____

My great-grandfather was born in

_____ on _____.
   (city/town)   (state)   (country)   (date)

If born outside the United States:

   His nationality was _____.

   His first language was _____.

   He grew up in _____.

   If he came to America, when did he arrive? _____

   Where? _____

Place and date my great-grandparents were married: _____

When my grandmother was born they lived in

_____.
   (city/town)   (state)   (country)

My Great-Grandparents
(Dad's Side)

(MY PATERNAL GRANDFATHER'S PARENTS)

My grandfather's parents' names: _____

My great-grandmother was born in

_____ on _____.
  (city/town)   (state)   (country)   (date)

If born outside the United States:

    Her nationality was _____.

    Her first language was _____.

    She grew up in _____.

    If she came to America, when did she arrive? _____

    Where? _____

My great-grandfather was born in

_____ on _____.
  (city/town)   (state)   (country)   (date)

If born outside the United States:

    His nationality was _____.

    His first language was _____.

    He grew up in _____.

    If he came to America, when did he arrive? _____

    Where? _____

Place and date my great-grandparents were married: _____

When my grandfather was born they lived in

_____.
  (city/town)   (state)   (country)

Family
Grab Bag

———●———

The Kind of Work We Do

FAMILY MEMBER   JOBS

My mom _____

My dad _____

Uncles _____

Aunts _____

My dad's parents _____

My mom's parents _____

Our relatives worked as: (Check all that apply.)

____ salespeople   ____ photographers
____ miners   ____ cooks
____ farmers   ____ butchers
____ engineers   ____ scientists
____ factory workers   ____ delivery people
____ mechanics   ____ storekeepers
____ cowboys   ____ sailors
____ merchants   ____ military men/women
____ teachers/professors   ____ nurses
____ lawyers   ____ politicians
____ doctors   ____ bakers
____ artists   ____ plumbers
____ carpenters   ____ tailors
____ actors   ____ waiters
____ singers   ____ peddlers
____ dancers   ____ blacksmiths
____ housekeepers   ____ railroad workers
____ writers   ____ fire fighters
____ artisans   ____ beauticians
____ secretaries   ____ construction workers
____ athletes   ____ bankers
____ electricians   ____ stockbrokers
____ cab drivers   ____ truck drivers
____ musicians   ____ computer technicians
____ diplomats   ____ police officers
____ editors   ____ other_____

Who Had What?

(Place check in each box that applies.)

	ME	MOM	DAD	GRAND-PARENTS	GREAT-GRANDPARENTS
Ice boxes					
Electricity					
Horse & carriages					
Cars					
Airplanes					
Refrigerators					
Radios					
Telephones					
Phonographs					
LP records					
45's					
Tape cassettes					
CD's					
VCR's					
Camcorders					
Black & white TV's					
Color TV's					
Panty hose					
Zippers					
Velcro					
Microwave ovens					
Car radios					
Pizza delivery					
Car phones					
Frozen foods					
Baby food in jars					
Disposable diapers					
Walkman					
Shopping malls					
Fax machines					
Personal computers					
Exercise shoes					
Nintendo					

Our Family Celebrations (Special Foods/Traditions/Rituals)

When a child is born we _____

_____

_____

_____.

Special growing-up events in our family include (baptisms, confirmations, bar mitzvahs, etc.): _____

_____

_____

_____.

When a person graduates we _____

_____

_____

_____.

On birthdays we _____

_____

_____

_____.

At weddings we _____

_____

_____

_____.

On anniversaries we _____

_____

_____

_____.

Family Holidays

On New Year's Eve we _____.

On New Year's Day we _____.

On Martin Luther King, Jr., Day we _____.

On Valentine's Day we _____.

On St. Patrick's Day we _____.

On Easter we _____.

On Passover we _____.

On Ramadan we _____.

On Memorial Day we _____.

On July 4th we _____.

On Labor Day we _____.

On Columbus Day we _____.

On Halloween we _____.

On Thanksgiving we _____.

On Christmas/Hanukkah/Kwanzaa we _____

_____

_____

_____.

Other holidays we celebrate and what we do: _____

_____

_____

_____

_____

Family What's What

If I were going to describe my family in five words, they would be _____

_____.

I'll never forget the day my family _____

_____

_____.

A value my family really believes in is _____

_____

_____.

My family is most proud of me when I _____

_____

_____.

I wish my family were more _____

_____

_____.

I wish my family were less _____

_____

_____.

If I could change my family in some way, it would be _____

_____

_____.

My family often _____

_____.

My family never _____

_____.

The happiest day for my family was _____

_____.

My family's favorite way to celebrate is _____

_____.

Family Who's Who

Kindest relatives: _____
_____

Best-educated relatives: _____
_____
_____

Best dancers: _____
_____

Best storytellers: _____
_____
_____

Relatives who are most fun: _____
_____

Best athletes: _____
_____
_____

Relatives who have pets: _____
_____
_____
_____
_____

Relatives with unusual hobbies: _____
_____
_____
_____
_____
_____

Tallest relative: _____

Shortest relative: _____

Youngest relative: _____

Oldest relative: _____

Most lovable relative: _____

Relatives who love their work: _____
_____

Relatives who grow (or grew) their own food: _____
_____
_____

Relatives who can ride horses: _____
_____

Relatives who have most recently arrived in America: _____
_____

Relatives who are twins: _____
_____

Relatives who are good cooks: _____
_____

Relatives who like to read: _____
_____

Relatives who always know what to do: _____

Relatives who always make us laugh: _____

Relatives who have had the biggest impact on me: _____
_____

Relatives I most want to be like when I grow up: _____
_____

Pictures of Me

Paste in one or two baby pictures
and one or two recent snapshots.

A Family Picture

Paste in a picture or draw a picture of your entire family, including any pets. Underneath or on the side of the picture, write in the name of each person and how he or she is related to you. Also write in the names of any pets. If you live with aunts, uncles, grandparents, or family friends, include them, too.

More Pictures

Paste in or draw more pictures of your
family doing the things your family likes to do.

Great Scraps

On the following pages paste important family memories. Things you might like to include: copies of birth certificates, an announcement of your birth or your parents' births, a ration book from World War II, interesting postcards with interesting messages, your report cards or one of your parent's report cards, dance cards, invitations to parties, wedding announcements, important family announcements in newspapers or magazines, favorite family recipes, etc.

Great Scraps

Great Scraps

Great Scraps

Great Scraps